FOR

Books by Rachel Pollack

Fiction

Temporary Agency (1994)
Godmother Night (1996)
Burning Sky (1998)
A Secret Woman (2002)
The Tarot Of Perfection (2008)

Non-fiction

78 Degrees Of Wisdom, parts 1 and 2 (1980 And 1983)
Salvador Dali's Tarot (1985)
Teach Yourself Fortune Telling (1986)
The Open Labyrinth (1986)
The New Tarot (1989)
The Haindl Tarot (1990)
Le Jeu Divinatoire (1991, France only)
Shining Woman Tarot Deck (1992)
The Vertigo Tarot (1995)
The Body Of The Goddess (1997)
Fabrications (1997)
The Haindl Tarot Workbook (1998)
Complete Illustrated Guide To The Tarot (1999)
The Power Of Ritual (2000)
Shining Tribe Tarot (2001)
The Forest of Souls (2003)
The Kabbalah Tree (2004)
Seeker (2006)
Tarot Wisdom (2008)

Anthologies

Tarot Tales (1989), Edited with Caitlin Matthewss

FORTUNE'S LOVERS

A BOOK OF TAROT POEMS

RACHEL POLLACK

FABULA RASA 02

A MIDSUMMER NIGHT'S PRESS

New York

A Midsummer Night's Press
16 West 36th Street
2ns Floor
New York, NY 10018
amidsummernightspress@gmail.com
www.amidsummernightspress.com

Designed by Marróndediseño *www.quintatinta.com.*

First edition, May 2009.

ISBN-13: 978-0-9794208-4-9
ISBN-10: 0-9794208-4-9

Printed in Spain.

for Frankie Greene

CONTENTS

FOOL

Out of Nothing comes Magic.
Out of Magic comes Silence.
Out of Silence comes Passion.
Out of Passion comes the flow
of earth between
heaven and birth.

Tight in a New York apartment, on
chairs and pillows and piano bench
twenty-five stories over
Second Avenue, in sight of a
gold-domed church,
with couch and plants and chairs and keys scented
with tobacco from pipe ceremonies and cigarettes,
we sat, squeezed together, eighteen of us,
(the Moon's number, Our Lady
of Lunacy, the Fool's mistress),
the last class in an herbalist's home,
and we talked about
the beginning, the breath, the opening,
the Fool.

We talked of early decks,

of "Fou," madness, how
the bright beautiful boy at the birth of the world
was once a schizophrenic homeless guy,
bitten by cats, desolation without end.
We talked of emptiness, of Nothing, of the open mouth
of Aleph, silent letter, Cantor's infinity, Jorge's
window to everything, the breath
before the thunder.
We remembered Fool stories, ancient and modern,
our own and others, and we talked
of how he lures us, and agreed
we could never live that way,
a dance without a self.
Then it ended, and I could see
The Hermit's hourglass, reminding me
that train schedules for country girls
going home are ruled by Emperors,
with no elastic Fool of time.

Down in the street, 34th and 2nd,
five lanes of traffic
pushing west. And across
the lanes a lone taxi waiting for green—
medallion 7022,
7 the Chariot, 0 the Fool, 22 the whole story—
my taxi, and soon it would turn and vanish. And so
I ran into the road.

Halfway across I heard the screams.
Wordless sounds of fear, amazement.
Five lanes of cars and trucks and
one tall woman, surprised as anyone.
No cars stopped, or even tried.
No shrill brakes, no shouts or horns,
this was New York, they just kept going.
And so did I, all the way across
34th Street to my Fool's chariot,
and a quiet ride
to the Emperor's train.

MAGICIAN

That which is below is like that which is above,
And that which is above is like that which is below,
To accomplish the miracles of one thing.

I call my brother Hermes,
My soul thief music man,
My dress up dancing man.

The Sun is its father.
The Moon is its mother.

I whistle him to come to me,
Sliding up the evening,
Dripping honey lies and magic.

The wind carried it in its belly.
The earth received and nourished it.

Hermes the con man,
Handing timeshares and cruises,
Guidebooks and theater passes,
Power points and promises,
To lackluster dead.

Separate Earth from Fire, subtle from gross,
Gently, with great prudence.

Hermes——my razzle dazzle mambo boy,
My scoundrel snake stick lover man,
Skin bags full of moly,
Stones and shiny feathers.

This is the power of powers,
For it overcomes all subtle things
And penetrates all solid things.

My sandal whisper gossip god,
My story serpent mojo man.

Thus the world is created,
The little world
According to the prototype,
The Great World.

My brother!
My Hermes!

Finished and perfect is what I have said,
The work of the Sun.

Excerpts from The Emerald Tablet of Hermes Trismegistus translated by Christopher Bamford

HIGH PRIESTESS

Of what?
That's what she asked her mother
when she got the job, with
the pretty robe, the vermeil crown, the sharp moon
tucked under her feet, and
the neatly lettered scroll she can never
seem to open.
Of what?
But her mother was one of the Old Ladies,
and that's just the sort of thing
they never answer.

So now when they come,
the men in the fur hats,
or the long black dresses with
the high white collars,
she can only stare,
and look impressive,
and hope they don't expect
some blessing or curse or detailed instructions for
making candles or killing goats.

Sometimes she imagines she's somewhere else,
on a camel, traveling by pricks of light,
searching for a man whose name
is laughter waiting outside
his mother's tent—
or regurgitating webs from a swollen belly—
or hanging from a hook
in her sister's meat locker
on the other side
of seven doors.

But she knows, unless
her mother of a thousand names
sends someone else
she will never leave this place,
the black and white columns,
the blue curtain, heavy
with palms and pomegranates,
hiding nothing but
a placid pool of water,
the tight scroll that tells her nothing,
and in her heart and in her face
no thunderspeak, no shining whisper,
only Silence.

EMPRESS

Four rabbis entered Paradise: ben Azzai, ben Zoma,
ben Abbuyah, and Rabbi Akiva. Ben Azzai looked into
the fire and died. Ben Zoma saw the waters above
and the waters below, and only three fingersbreadth
between them, and was lost to reason. Ben Abbuyah
saw two thrones in heaven, not one, and became
an enemy of his people. Only Rabbi Akiva entered
and left in peace.

An old story

Really—it's not very complicated,
not some mind-twister, like
I, the LORD your God, am a jealous God...
Here—listen:
"If a bird's nest chance to be before you with fledglings or eggs,
                    you shall
set aside the mother, so that you will enjoy length of days."
And now here's another one:
"Honor your father and your mother, so that
you will enjoy length of days."
So, that's it, two places in the whole Book,
and each of them as simple, really,
as eat your oatmeal.

Except—
Here's what the later teachers say about that bird's nest.
The bird is Binah, sephirah number 3
                (like card 3, the Empress)
      on the Tree of Life,
the Great Mother
                (like the Empress),
the Source
                ("out of the Three come the Ten Thousand Things").
And the nest—not some bowl of twigs and bird spit, but
Paradise itself, Eden, home of two big trees and four rivers.
How did something simple get so complicated?
Why not leave it as
Be nice to birds and have a good life?

There was once a man
named Elisha ben Abuyyah,
an early rabbi, a mind like a hurricane,
back when the Romans destroyed the temple
and were hunting Jews.
This was the beginning,
when the rabbis were creating a world
out of stories and morals instead of
temple gates and sacrificed goats.

Two winds blew at Elisha,
Torah and philosophy, the Jew and the Greek,

Akiva and Aristotle.
In that story of the four,
ben Abbuyah was the best of them,
the smartest, yet deep
in the valley of doubt.
When he decided One God was a lie,
he didn't just walk away, he
turned in his friends to the Romans,
as if Malcolm X, say, had fingered his pals
to the FBI. You can guess the results.
Was it really just a meditation gone bad?

Here's another version.
Elisha was out walking when
he saw a man with a boy
alongside a tree.
"See that nest up there?"
the man told his son.
"Climb up and bring me down some eggs."
The boy stared at the plump bird
and the thin branch.
"Abba," he said, "I can't go up there,
the tree won't hold me."
"I'm your father!" the man said, blind
for an omelet. "You'll do what I say."
The boy climbed the tree,
gently urged aside the squawking mother,

removed a pair of eggs, and on the way down
broke a branch, and fell
to his death.
Did his Abba scream and beat his chest?
Nobody knows. But Elisha ben Abbuyah—
It's all a lie roared in his mind.
He stared from the broken-necked boy
to his friends, all rabbis and students, and
told them, *He did the only two things in the whole book
that promise you a long life. And now he's dead!*
They said, Maybe it means the Afterlife,
maybe he already prospers in the World On High.
But Elisha ben Abbuyah had already walked away,
swept in a storm
to the Other Side.

Out of that moment comes
all Kabbalah, all its trees and lines and circles,
all its diagrams and glory,
people transformed into emanations,
laws into allegories, bird into Empress—
all to make sure that
what happened to the hurricane mind
of Elisha ben Abbuyah
never happens again.

EMPEROR

Once upon a time there was
a little girl—a princess,
or so she thought.
Seven, eight, I don't
remember now.
She came home to the castle
one day, crying, snuffling,
the whole routine.
Her father, the all-powerful King,
dropped his pipe and newspaper,
and sat her on his lap, where he
wiped away her tears.
Or so she expected.

Instead, Daddy kept his hands
on the Globe, and
only asked, "What's wrong?"
"Billy hit me!" the princess said, with
gulps of tears.
Now, she thought, now the King
would show his Knightly side, and
slay the wicked Billy.
"Did you hit him back?" her father asked.

Well. *This* was unexpected.
All the princess could do
was answer "No."
"Why not?" her father asked.
More surprise. She knew
she had to think quickly.
"He's bigger than me," she said, certain now
that she had found the magic formula to
transform her lumpen father into
a noble champion.
"You could use a stick,"
her daddy said.
A pause followed, just a couple of seconds,
but a span of years in fairy time,
long enough for the princess hat,
long and pointy,
to change into a hero's lance.
From that moment, the former princess told me,
she never looked to any man
to protect or fight for her.

LOVERS

He was out walking with the sheep
when he saw the snakes,
two of them, copulating. He pushed his
staff, his Ace of Wands,
between them and became, briefly,
the Caduceus, a spine of light
entwined with serpents.
And when the human stepped back she'd
become a woman.
Seven years passed, as she traveled
through the seven planetary spheres,
the seven palaces supported on seven wise pillars.
Then she saw the snakes again,
the same pair or another, it makes no difference,
she moved her Cup between them,
and became—
not a man again, but something
more, beyond addition and subtraction,
a Knower, a Speaker,
blinded by Hera, sighted by Zeus,
Teiresias, whose name means
The One Who Delights In Signs.

The card of the Lovers—
a man on the right, a woman on the left,
and above and between them an angel
with outstretched arms and fiery hair—
together they are all Teiresas,
bright Caduceus in a single life.

A PRAISE POEM FOR TEIRESIAS

Delighter in signs, ancestor,
you are always right.
You see beyond sight.
You see all the way through.
Delighter in signs, ancestor,
you read correctly.

Delighter in signs, ancestor,
You are always right.
Your body is snakes,
your face is wings,
your hair is plumage.
Delighter in signs, ancestor,
you question the owls,
they cannot refuse you.

Delighter of signs, ancestor,

you read correctly.
You know the secrets of men,
you know the secrets of women,
you know between and beyond,
above and below.
Delighter of signs, ancestor,
you taste the tongues of angels.

Delighter of signs, ancestor,
you are always right.
You open the door,
you see beyond windows.
You know all the meanings,
you know reversed and upright,
you know all the spreads.
Delighter of signs, ancestor,
you read correctly.

WHEEL OF FORTUNE

A king in white and red—
old hair and ermine shoulders,
face flush with power—
sits in a gold chair atop
a twelve-spoked wheel.
The wheel shifts—
sometimes a woman, or an upright bear,
turns a crank, and sometimes
the wheel just follows its nature—
and because the king has forgotten
how to leave his throne
he ends up crushed
at the bottom,
all his golden power washed in blood
that dyes and mats his ermine glory.
King Arthur saw this,
held in a dream the night before
his bastard incest son
devoured his imperial vision.
This is mortal time,
the repetitive truth.

Look—the first *tarocchi* deck,
the gold-infused Visconti-Sfroza—
there he is, on top of the Wheel,
a young king, golden-haired,
holding out an open palm,
as if to offer grace,
and there again, his future,
old and broken,
at the bottom.
Only, the boy on top
wears donkey ears. Is he
a carnival monarch? Or is every ruler,
every hero, and every peasant
a King of Fools?
And in the center,
somehow like a character
from a country-western song,
stands a blindfolded angel
hands resting on the spokes.
This is time's mysteries,
unknown and certain all at once.

In the sixteenth century *Tarot de Marseille*
animals crowd the Wheel.
Devotion's dog climbs the right side,
a scramble up
towards light, and on the left,

a monkey stalks head first
down the rough wood Wheel, pulled
by hunger, lust, confusion.
No angel now, but a crowned sphinx,
a sword set rakishly on her shoulder.
This is evolution's time, not Darwin
or Lamarck, but shifts of
self and body, over and over,
as the Big Wheel keeps on turning.

We who read cards
are Fortune's lovers,
intoxicated by other people's lives,
their memories like dreams we live in pictures,
their starts and detours and dead ends,
their round and round and round,
like a thick liquer.
Their mistakes and triumphs spark in us
a shameless joy of images.
This is time illumined,
St. Catherine's wheel of lives,
sweet Fortune's gift.

HANGED MAN

A STORY OF MERLIN

It happened in his early days,
before the elder wise man gig, the
young king with his twelve disciples,
and long before he let his secretary
lock him in a cave.
Back then he lived in Wales,
and for a time in the woods,
a Hermit Fool, astray,
like Sweeney, eating twigs
and talking to owls.
Then one day, something
drove him sane, and he
returned, a grass-stained magic man,
to court, where his sister ruled as Queen.
Awkwardly, her royal husband welcomed
his famous lunatic brother-in-law.
Merlin laughed, slapped his torn robe in glee.
"Merlin?" said the King, "You want to share the joke?"
"Sure," Merlin said, banking his glee to a snicker.
"You're married to her—" pointing his raw beard
at his sister, "but she's sleeping with

tall, dark, and muscled over there." His long
finger marked a would-be Lancelot
who started reaching for his sword.
The Queen said, "How can you listen to him?
He's crazy. He sits in trees and
talks to owls."
Silence.
"Look," the Queen said, "I can prove it."
She grabbed a Page, held him
like him a trophy, said
"Tell me, wise prophet, how
will this boy die?"
Merlin smiled, bits of leaves
showing in his teeth.
"He will fall from a high place."
The Queen rushed the boy from the room,
cut his hair, changed his clothes, yanked him back.
"And how will *this* boy die?"
"He will die by hanging," the Magician said.
Laughter, whistles, and the king felt
the horns shrinking on his head.
Once again the Queen took away the Page,
threw a dress over his head,
a veil over his face.
"And this one?" she said.
Merlin looked around the room, nodded
at the audience. "Girl or no," he said,

"this one will die by drowning."
Uproar. Cheers. "You see?"
crowed the Queen, "he's no seer,
he's a Fool!"
Years later, a Knight who was once a
costume-switching Page, was out
hunting with his dog. A white hart
entranced him, and without looking,
like a very Fool, he
stepped off a cliff.
Down he fell, head first, like
a fetus leaving its mother.
He would have cracked his skull, except
his foot caught in a tree,
just right, it seems, to
immerse his head
in a rushing river—
a Hanged Man, with
three dark doors
to shiny Death.

after The Merlin Tarot, by R. J. Stewart

DEVIL

1.

Adam was off somewhere naming.
Oh, how he loved to name,
told Eve the sounds he gave
to this one, or that one—
cougar, aardvark, hippopotamus—
were the truth, and gave him
power over them, by the Creator's design.
But Eve knew the Creator had just given Adam the job
to see what he would say. When God had
paraded everything before him,
when the final insect had buzzed,
Adam stood at the edge of
the garden, staring at
the river, or up among the leaves, hoping
he could find something he hadn't named, something
the Creator had forgotten.
So Eve was alone, resting
against a tree, holding a pomegranate,
and counting its seeds,
when Mr. Dark and Shiny came, strolling
through the grass. Later, Eve figured out he must have
found a back door, or a hole in the fence.

He wore a green zoot suit,
with pearl buttons, and real-looking
eyes that winked at her from the points
of the shoulders, and a wide black hat
to keep the sun off his face.
And shoes—slithery snakeskin with polished brass toes.
Eve had never seen clothes before,
let alone anything like this.
"Has Adam named you?" she said.
"No," he said, "I'm Samael."
She held out the pomegranate. When he
bit it, the juices squirted
down his chin, long and knobbly, and
some of it splashed on Eve, her mouth,
her belly, between her legs.
"Let me clean you," he said,
but then he pierced right into her,
slamming her back against
the trunk of the tree.

2.

Adam was dreaming.
His great invention, he called it,
though he also said an angel named Raziel
had given him instructions, a Book of Secrets,
stolen from heaven.
Adam didn't like angels, they all
had names before he got to them
(like the snake, and the sea, and the
Tree of Fire and the Tree No One Was Allowed To Touch,
all of which the Creator had named
before Adam got started).
He didn't like angels, but he liked his book, and
he liked dreams. He said they gave him
new creatures to name, a fresh start every night.
While Adam dreamt, something
was happening to Eve. Her belly
got round and hard, and inside
she could feel something, with parts
that moved and hurt her, as if it was trying
to kick its way out.
She made herself vomit,
but it was too far down. She hoped
that when the Moon filled up,
her blood would carry away

whatever was hurting her. But
the thing inside must have drunk
all her blood, because nothing came out.
The Moon went away and came back, and
went away and came back, she lost track
of how many times, and Adam
was dreaming, and studying secrets,
and only the snake
would comfort her, wrapping around
the ball of her body
as she leaned back against a Tree she vaguely
remembered she was not supposed to touch.
"Please," she told the snake,
"get it out of me." The snake
squeezed and let go, squeezed and let go,
and suddenly a small head,
slimy and blood-soaked, appeared
between her legs, and with one final
kick, it broke loose from her,
and she was free.

3.

Adam was thrilled.
Something new to name, and
he didn't have to dream it,
or lose it when he woke up.
"It looks like me" he said,
"only smaller." And wetter, with flashes
of darkness that moved across its skin
and hurt Adam's eyes as he tried to name it.
Nothing came to him. He picked it up, turned it
round and round, poked it with his thumb.
It made a noise, a sound like the sea,
rising and falling, but high and angry, over and over, until
Adam dropped it to cover his ears.
"Make it stop!" he ordered Eve, and said
"No wonder I can't find its name. All that noise. I
can't think, how can I name if I can't think?"
Eve picked it up, stroked it, made soft noises at it,
held out a fruit for food or a toy. It wouldn't stop.
She tried to push it back inside her. It
twisted and kicked, and the noise got louder.
Adam broke a branch from the Tree,
sharpened the edge against a stone, and
drove it through the creature's chest.
"There!" he said, "how can I name

with all that noise?" Thinking,
a creature he couldn't name
did not deserve to live.
But the noise didn't stop, became
more steady, a pulse uninterrupted by breath.
Adam grabbed a second branch,
with both hands stabbed and chopped it,
ten pieces, twenty, and the noise broke apart,
sounding like a surge of hornets stinging
every part of him. "Please," he begged
his wife, "make it stop."
Eve filled a giant shell with river water,
added fruit from the Tree You Mustn't Touch,
then the shrieking pieces of meat,
then carried the whole thing to the
Tree of Fire, where she set it down among the roots.
As the water heated up, the cries came
softer and softer, like the slow death of a storm.
With a smaller shell Adam scooped out
the tender pieces, the boiled fruit. "I name
this *dinner*" he said, and laughed as he ate.
Now Eve joined him, so hungry she just
used her hands, and even immersed her face
in the hot broth. Soon it was gone, every piece, and
all they could do was sit on the dirt,
and watch sparks shoot from the Tree of Fire, back
to the Tree They Were Never Supposed To Touch.

4.

Here comes Samael,
face all shiny, pearl buttons so bright
the leaves wince and curl away.
"Where's my son?" he says,
"Where's my precious boy?"
Adam says, "I don't know what you mean."
Samael stands straighter, and all the plants stiffen into claws.
"Give me my son!" he bellows.
Eve steps back and covers her mouth, in case
she's forgotten to wipe away the juice,
or any bits of meat.
"I don't understand," she says.
Small rocks shoot up from the dirt,
and she and Adam cling to the Tree.
A voice speaks, thin and sweet, from
inside their bellies and along their veins.
             "Father," it says, "you can go home now.
They have taken me into their mouths,
and deep in their hearts, and I will
stay with them, and all their children, and all
their children's children, forever after,
for as long as the life of the Tree."

from a Yemenite Jewish folk tale

WORLD

YIHUD
Yearning Ignites Holy Unknown Desire

Yihud is Hebrew for Union. In the 16th century the great Kabbalist mystic, Isaac Luria, created a series of *yihudim*, prayers and spiritual exercises ultimately designed to re-unite the pieces of a broken universe, even the sundered male and female aspects of God. The female bears the name *Shekhinah*, literally "indwelling presence." In Tarot tradition, the Shekinah is the World.

For the life of the Union
Of the First and the Last,
The Crown and Shekhinah—

The Broken and the Perfect
The Body and the Infinite
The Image and the Act
The Winged and the Dirt—

For the perfect restoration
Of dismembered souls,
Our scattered pieces,
Sparks struck
In mountain and wave,

Music and snow,
The eye and the tongue—

I, Rachel,
Daughter of Pictures,
Daughter of Names—

Sister of Wings,
Of Shekhinah Ruach HaOlam,
Presence, Breath of the World—

I offer myself,
Synapse and skin,
To the mitzvoth of the beloved—

You shall love the Eternal,
Your Mother,
With all your heart and all your might—
You shall love your fellow being
As yourself—

And by this grace,
May I open up my mouth.

TAROT PI

This poem was generated by translating the numbers 0-9 into words related to the first ten cards of the Tarot Major Arcana (along with "Awakens" for the decimal point). The words were then substituted for their numbers in the first hundred digits of the irrational number known as Pi. Pi represents the ratio of any circle's circumference to its diameter, which is always 22/7. Twenty-two is the number of cards in the complete Major Arcana. Seven is the number of colors in the rainbow, the chakras in the human body, and the "planetary spheres" of ancient cosmology. If you divide 22 by 7, you get a number that begins 3.14 and goes on forever, never resolving itself, and never repeating any sustained sequence. The first hundred digits of Pi are **3.1415926535 8979323846 2643383279 5028841971 6939937510 5820974944 5923078164 0628620899 8628034825 34 21170679**

0 *(Fool)* Reckless
1 *(Magician)* Light
2 *(High Priestess)* Silence
3 *(Empress)* Pleasure
4 *(Emperor)* Power
5 *(Hierophant)* Blessing
6 *(Lovers)* Desire
7 *(Chariot)* Rolling
8 *(Strength)* Lion
9 *(Hermit)* Lonely
. Awakens

Pleasure awakens light,
power light
blessing lonely silence.
Desire blessing pleasure. Desire
lion lonely rolling pleasure, silence pleasure.
Lion power, desire silence, desire power.
Pleasure pleasure, lion pleasure. Silence.
Rolling lonely blessing,
reckless silence.
Lion, lion, power light,
lonely rolling light.
Desire lonely pleasure,
lonely, lonely pleasure.
Rolling blessing light, reckless
blessing. Lion silence, reckless
lonely rolling power,
lonely power,
power blessing lonely silence
pleasure. Reckless
rolling lion, light desire power. Reckless
desire, silence, lion desire silence. Reckless
lion, lonely lonely lion, desire silence lion. Reckless
pleasure, power lion.
Silence blessing pleasure.
Power silence light, light
rolling reckless desire,
rolling lonely.

FOOL

The wise man hears of the Gate
and studies the lock every day.
The devotee hears of the Gate
and tries to squeeze between the bars.
The fool hears of the Gate
and laughs. Without laughter
the Gate would never open.

RACHEL POLLACK (Brooklyn, 1945) is the author of thirty books of fiction and non-fiction, most recently *Tarot Wisdom* and *Tarot of Protection*. She is a poet, an award-winning novelist, an authority on the modern interpretation of Tarot cards, and a Tarot card artist.

Her novel *Godmother Night* won the 1997 World Fantasy Award and was described by Kirkus Reviews as "a magical exploration of the deepest roots of life and death." Her earlier novel, *Unquenchable Fire,* won Britain's Arthur C. Clarke Award, and was described by *The New York Review of Science Fiction* as "not only the best fantasy of the year, possibly the best of the decade, and the best feminist novel of the decade." Her non-fiction book, *Seeker,* won the COVR Award for best book on divination at the 2006 International New Age Trade Show.

She has published fifteen books on Tarot and divination, including *78 Degrees of Wisdom,* considered a modern classic and "the Bible of Tarot reading." She also has written on other non-fiction subjects, including *The Body of the Goddess,* which traces the origin and development of religion in the human body and nature.

She is also a visual artist; she is the creator of *The Shining Tribe Tarot,* which she wrote and illustrated herself.

Her books have been published in fourteen languages.

She teaches in the MFA program at Goddard College.

A MIDSUMMER NIGHT'S PRESS was founded by Lawrence Schimel in New Haven, CT in 1991. Using a letterpress, it published broadsides of poems by Nancy Willard, Joe Haldeman, and Jane Yolen, among others, in signed, limited editions of 126 copies, numbered 1-100 and lettered A-Z. One of the broadsides— "Will" by Jane Yolen—won a Rhysling Award. In 1993, the publisher moved to New York and the press went on hiatus until 2007, when it began publishing perfect-bound, commercially-printed books under three imprints:

FABULA RASA: devoted to works inspired by mythology, folklore, and fairy tales. The first titles from this imprint are *Fairy Tales for Writers* by Lawrence Schimel and *Fortune's Lover: A Book of Tarot Poems* by Rachel Pollack.

FUNNY BONES: devoted to works of humor and light verse. The first titles from this imprint are *The Good-Neighbor Policy,* a murder mystery told in double dactyls by Edgar Award-winner Charles Ardai, and the forthcoming anthology of clerihews, *Irreverent Biographies.*

BODY LANGUAGE: devoted to texts exploring questions of gender and sexual identity. The first titles from this imprint are *This is What Happened in Our Other Life,* the first collection of poems from Lambda Literary Award-winner Achy Obejas; *Banalities* by Brane Mozetic, translated from the Slovene by Elizabeta Zargi with Timothy Liu; and the annual anthology series *Best Gay Poetry* and *Best Lesbian Poetry.*